I0828193

THIS BOOK BELONGS TO:

WELCOME TO MICHIGAN

Dedicated to all the explorers.

ISBN 978-1-958985-95-3

www.joeysavestheday.com

Mimi Books™ Publishing

A Mimi Book

Michigan's name comes from the Indigenous peoples who lived around the Great Lakes long before European explorers arrived. The word comes from the Ojibwe term "mishigami," which means "big lake" or "great water."

Because the region is surrounded by some of the largest lakes in the world, early French explorers began using this Native word on their maps. Over time, it grew into the name Michigan, the state we know today.

Michigan's history begins with Native American nations who lived around the Great Lakes for thousands of years. French explorers arrived in the 1600s, followed by the British, and Michigan later became part of the United States. In the early 1900s, Michigan became famous for building cars, helping shape modern transportation. Today, it's known for its lakes, forests, and rich past.

Michigan was the twenty-sixth state to join the Union. It officially joined on January 26, 1837.

26th

Michigan is in the East North Central region of the United States. It borders Ohio, Indiana, and Wisconsin, and it also touches Ontario, Canada, across the Great Lakes. The state is surrounded by Lake Superior, Lake Michigan, Lake Huron, and Lake Erie, giving it the longest freshwater coastline in the nation.

Lansing is the capital of Michigan.
It officially became the state capital in 1847.

Detroit, Michigan, has an estimated population of about 645,700 people.
Michigan

Michigan is the eleventh largest state in the United States by area.

Grand Rapids, Michigan

There are approximately 10,000,000 people residing in the state of Michigan.

Jackson, Michigan

In downtown Holland, Michigan, there's a bronze statue of Benjamin Franklin sitting on a bench with the Declaration of Independence in his hand. Franklin was born in Boston, Massachusetts, on January 17, 1706, and became one of America's most creative Founding Fathers. The statue was made in 1991, and kids love it because you can sit right beside "Ben" for a fun photo.

Michigan is known for its tasty cherries, especially the bright red ones grown around Traverse City. These cherries are sweet, juicy, and perfect for making pies, jams, and other yummy treats. Families all across Michigan enjoy them during festivals, holidays, and summertime gatherings, and cherries have become one of the state's most beloved and iconic foods.

MICHIGAN

There are 83 counties in Michigan.

Here is a list of twenty of those counties:

Alcona	Branch	Eaton	Isabella
Alger	Calhoun	Emmet	Jackson
Allegan	Cass	Genesee	Kalamazoo
Alpena	Charlevoix	Gladwin	Kalkaska
Antrim	Cheboygan	Gogebic	Kent

Tahquamenon Falls is one of Michigan's most famous natural wonders, located deep in the forests of the Upper Peninsula. The Upper Falls is a huge, powerful waterfall that stretches almost 200 feet across and drops 50 feet into the river below. The water has a golden-brown color from the natural tannins in the surrounding cedar and hemlock trees, giving it the nickname "Root Beer Falls." A short drive away, the Lower Falls features several smaller cascades that flow around a peaceful island.

One of the coolest things in Michigan is the Detroit–Windsor Tunnel, which opened in 1930. It was the first underwater tunnel in the world that connected two different countries. The tunnel runs beneath the Detroit River and links Detroit, Michigan with Windsor, Ontario. When it opened, people were amazed that cars could drive under a river to reach another nation. Today, it is still an important border crossing and a fun reminder of Michigan's creative engineering history.

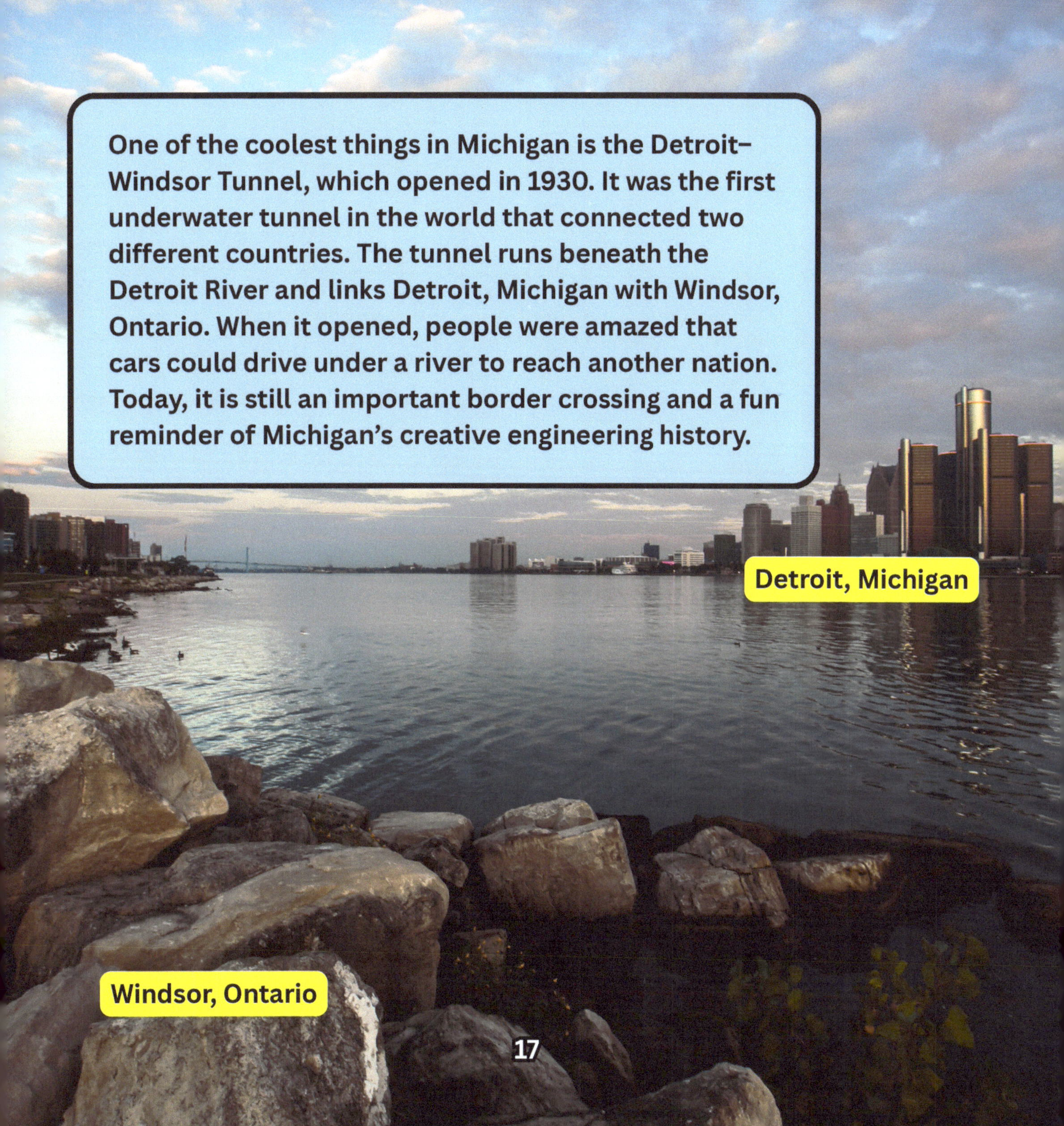

The Mackinac Bridge

The Mackinac Bridge stretches across the sparkling waters where Lake Michigan and Lake Huron meet, connecting Michigan's Upper and Lower Peninsulas. Opened in 1957, this mighty suspension bridge is one of the longest in the world and helps thousands of travelers, families, and trucks cross safely every day. With its tall towers and sweeping cables, the "Mighty Mac" is one of Michigan's most beloved landmarks.

The Michigan state bird is the American Robin. It was chosen as the state bird in 1931.

The official state flower of Michigan is the apple blossom. It was chosen as the state flower in 1897.

A couple of Michigan's nicknames include the Wolverine State and the Great Lakes State.

Lake Michigan

Michigan's motto is "Si Quaeris Peninsulam Amoenam Circumspice," which is Latin for "If you seek a pleasant peninsula, look about you."

What the motto means:

If you want to see a beautiful place, just look around Michigan.

BEAUTIFUL

The abbreviation for Michigan is MI.

MI

Michigan's state flag was officially adopted in 1911.

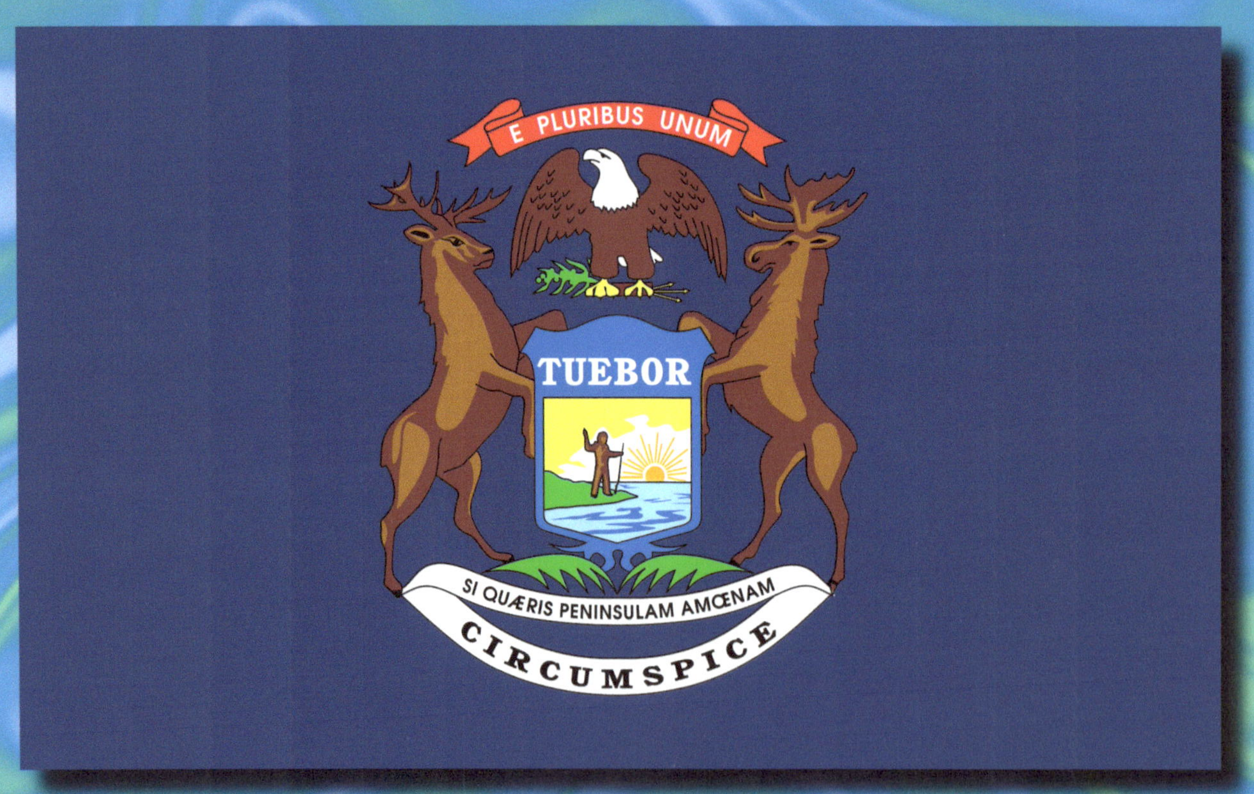

Some crops grown in Michigan are cherries, soybeans, apples, and wheat.

Some animals that live in Michigan are white-tailed deer, black bears, red foxes, beavers, and sandhill cranes.

Michigan experiences a wide range of temperatures throughout the year. The hottest temperature ever recorded in the state was 112 degrees Fahrenheit, measured in Mio on July 13, 1936. In contrast, the coldest temperature documented was −51 degrees Fahrenheit, recorded in Vanderbilt on February 9, 1934.

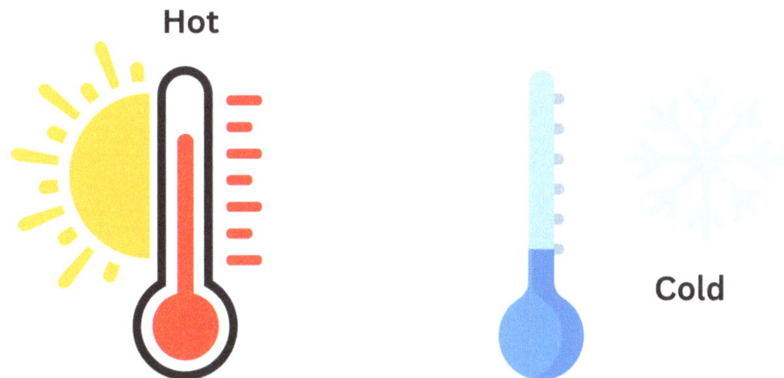

The Detroit Zoo in Royal Oak, Michigan, is a wonderful place to explore, with animals from all around the world. Kids can see lions, bears, giraffes, penguins, and playful primates, along with colorful birds and reptiles.

Michigan is called the Great Lakes State because it touches four of the five Great Lakes. Lake Superior, Lake Michigan, Lake Huron, and Lake Erie surround the state with miles of sparkling freshwater. These huge lakes help animals, shape the weather, and give Michigan more freshwater shoreline than any other state.

Lake Superior

Lake Michigan

Lake Huron

Lake Erie

The largest airport in Michigan is Detroit Metropolitan Wayne County Airport, located in Romulus, near Detroit. It sits at 11050 West G Rogell Drive and serves as the main travel hub for people flying in and out of Michigan. This airport connects travelers to cities across the country and to destinations around the world, making it one of the busiest and most important airports in the Midwest.

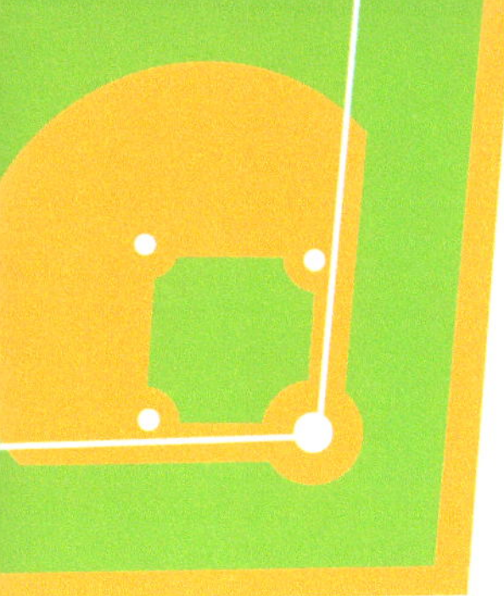

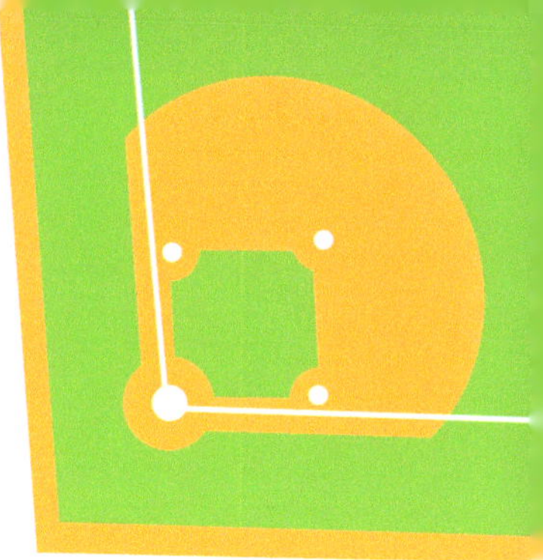

The Detroit Tigers are a Major League Baseball team based in Detroit, one of Michigan's most well-known cities. They play their home games at Comerica Park, a bright and lively ballpark known for its fun family atmosphere, giant tiger statues, and exciting scoreboard displays. The Tigers are one of the oldest teams in baseball, and many future major-league stars have played here as they built their skills and made baseball history.

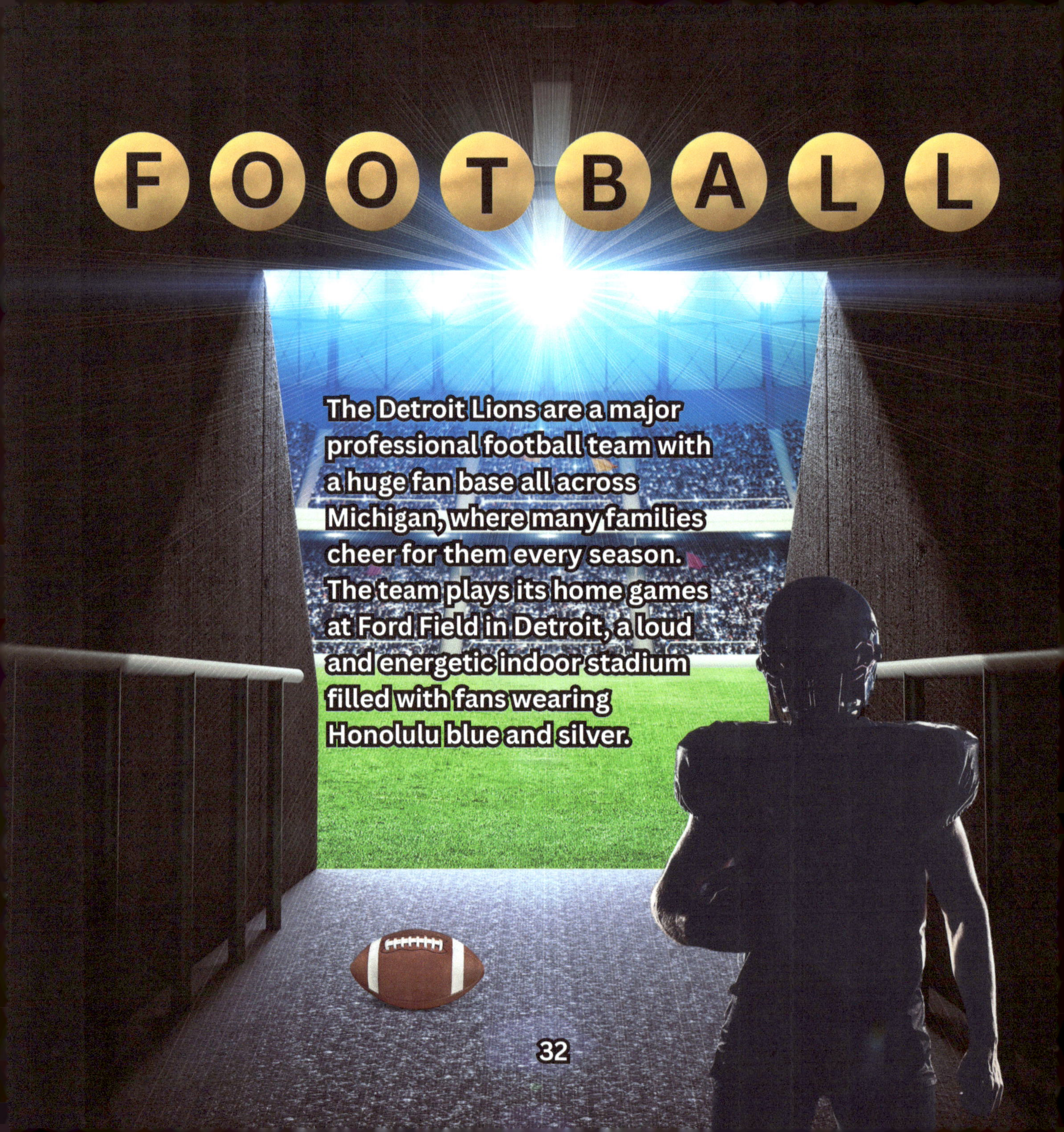

FOOTBALL

The Detroit Lions are a major professional football team with a huge fan base all across Michigan, where many families cheer for them every season. The team plays its home games at Ford Field in Detroit, a loud and energetic indoor stadium filled with fans wearing Honolulu blue and silver.

The eastern white pine is Michigan's state tree. It's known for its tall, straight trunk and soft, bluish-green needles that stay on the tree all year long. The eastern white pine was officially adopted as the state tree in 1955, and its towering shape and gentle needles have made it a beloved symbol of Michigan's forests and natural beauty.

The brook trout is Michigan's state fish. It's a small, colorful fish with bright spots and a shimmering pattern that make it easy to recognize in cool, clear streams. The brook trout was officially adopted as the state fish in 1988.

Can you name these?

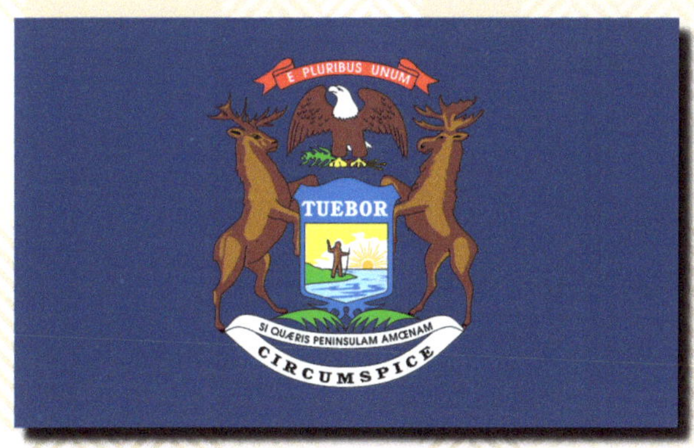

I hope you enjoyed
learning about
Michigan.

To explore fun facts about the other 49 states, visit my website at www.joeysavestheday.com. You'll also find a wide variety of homeschool resources to support joyful learning at home. If you enjoyed this book, I would be grateful if you left a review. Your feedback truly helps. Thank you for your support!

Check out these other interesting books in the
50 States Fact Books Series!

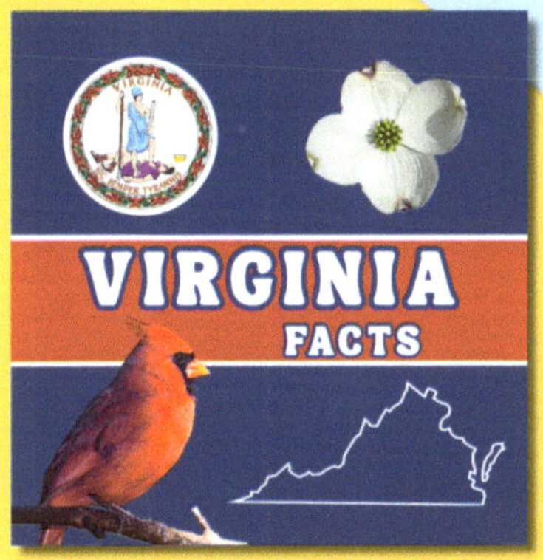

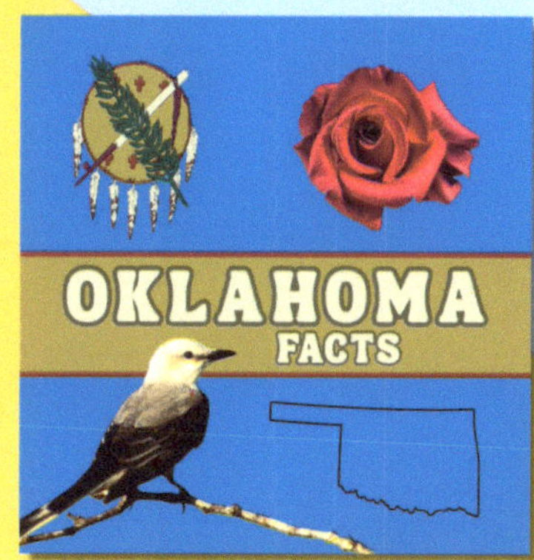

www.mimibooks.com

www.ingramcontent.com/pod-product-compliance
Lightning Source LLC
LaVergne TN
LVHW070200110826
845147LV00002B/457
* 9 7 8 1 9 5 8 9 8 5 9 5 3 *